MALE MENOPAWS

{The Silent Howl}

This book is dedicated to the memory of "Butchie,"
my best friend.

Acknowledgments:
Much appreciation to Andy for listening to me
all those months and for being a good friend.
Also many thanks to all the characters in my life
for their inspiration for this book.
Hugs and extra doggie biscuits to my
special boys: Tex, Jiggs, and King.

MALE MENOPAWS

{The Silent Howl}

by Marty Sacks

Illustrations by Jack E. Davis

Ten Speed Press
Berkeley, California

🔟

Ten Speed Press
P.O. Box 7123
Berkeley, CA 94707
www.tenspeedpress.com

A Kirsty Melville Book

Distributed in Australia by Simon and Schuster Australia, in Canada by Ten
Speed Press Canada, in New Zealand by Tandem Press, in South Africa by
Real Books, in Southeast Asia by Berkeley Books, and in the United
Kingdom and Europe by Airlift Books.

Cover and text design by Lisa Patrizio
Edited by Andy Meisler

**Library of Congress
Cataloging-in-Publication Data**
Sacks, Martha.
Male menopaws / by Martha Sacks;
illustrations by Jack E. Davis.
p. cm.
ISBN 0-89815-945-8 {alk. paper}
1. Dogs—Caricature and cartoons
2. Middle aged men—Caricature and cartoons
I. Title
PN6727.S15M45 1998
741.5'973–dc21
98-27374 CIP

Printed in Hong Kong

1 2 3 4 5 6 7 8 9 10 — 08 07 06 05 04 03 02 00 99 98

INTRODUCTION

Among medical and health experts, as well as among a new breed of psychologists, it's been a bone of contention for years: Do males experience a so-called "change of life"?

To many in need of additional training this is nothing more than a trick question. On the contrary: nearly everyone making the transition from young pup to mature adult undergoes important, sometimes drastic, changes.

Many males, of course, try to bury their problems as they arise. A better strategy is to learn how to unleash your fears, face them down, and put your best feet forward. Get your tail out from between your legs. Get back on the right path.

Heal!

PART I

YOUR BODY

8

REMEDY Acceptance

SYMPTOM   Change in body shape

REMEDY Better wardrobe

SYMPTOM   Eyesight changes

13

REMEDY Fashionable eyewear

14

SYMPTOM   **Loss of height**

REMEDY Custom furniture

SYMPTOM   Loss of sexual prowess

REMEDY Sexual aids

SYMPTOM Prostate trouble

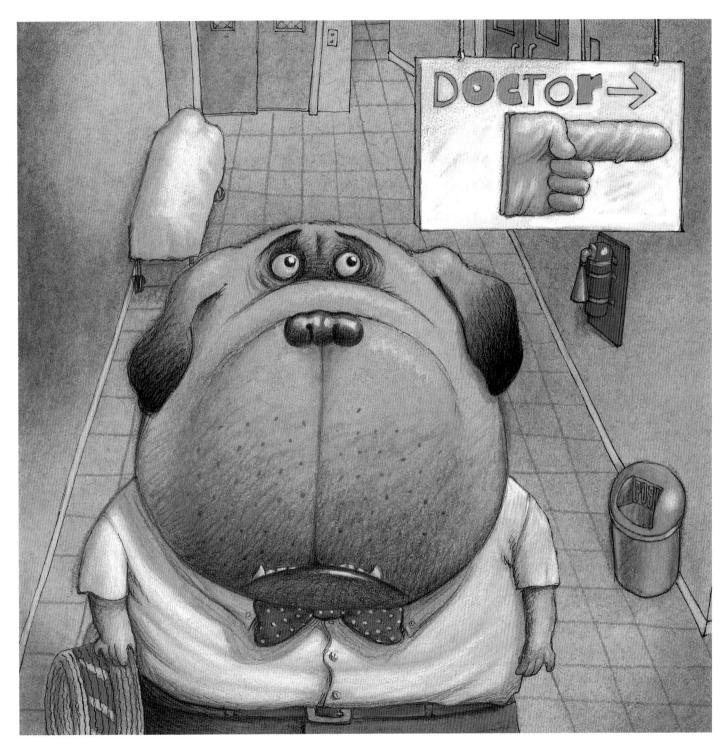

REMEDY Annual checkups

SYMPTOM   Decreased tolerance for alcohol

REMEDY Change in drinking habits

SYMPTOM   Bran addiction

REMEDY Support group

PART II

YOUR MIND

DIFFICULTY **Apathy**

STRATEGY Activism

DIFFICULTY Yearning for lost youth

STRATEGY   New friends

DIFFICULTY Obsession with danger

STRATEGY Virtual reality

DIFFICULTY **Obsessive fantasizing**

STRATEGY Reality

DIFFICULTY **Misanthropy**

STRATEGY   Philanthropy

DIFFICULTY **Indecisiveness**

STRATEGY   Sound decision-making techniques

DIFFICULTY **Insomnia**

STRATEGY   New hobbies

DIFFICULTY **Depression**

STRATEGY   Fishing!

PART III

YOUR LIFESTYLE

PROBLEM   Spiritual crisis

45

SOLUTION   Spiritual guidance

PROBLEM Job burnout

SOLUTION   Relaxation techniques

PROBLEM   Inappropriate career changes

AVERAGE LIFE EXPECTANCY

ACCOUNTANTS, LAWYERS, FROGMEN

49

SOLUTION   Career counseling

PROBLEM Ambivalence about retirement

SOLUTION   Part-time job

PROBLEM Fatalism

SOLUTION   **Futurism**

PROBLEM   Hypochondria

SOLUTION   Alternative therapies

PROBLEM   Great White Hunter syndrome

SOLUTION   **Bond with nature**

PROBLEM   Wanderlust

SOLUTION   Wander!

BIBLIOGRAPHY

{BOOKS}

Bednarik, Karl. **The Male in Crisis.** New York: Greenwood Publishing Group, 1981.

Block, Dave. **MMS-No Laughing Matter: Male Menopausal Syndrome.** Oklahoma City, Okla: Laid Back Enterprises, 1993.

Bly, Robert. **Iron John: A Book About Men.** New York: Vintage, 1992.

Brenton, Myron. **Aging Slowly.** Emmaus, Pa.: Rodale Press, 1984.

Cole, Joanna. **A Dog's Body.** New York: William Morrow, 1986.

Colen, B. **Meet Me in the Doghouse.** Garden City, N.Y.: Doubleday, 1973.

Danoff, Dudley Seth, and M. D. Danoff. **Superpotency: How to Get It, Use It, and Maintain It for a Lifetime.** New York: Warner Books, 1993.

Dodman, Nicholas H. **The Dog Who Loved Too Much: Tales, Treatments, and the Psychology of Dogs.** New York: Bantam, 1997.

Evans, Tripp. **Normal Men/Desperate Women.** New York: St. Martin's Press, 1989.

Feirstein, Bruce, and Lee Lorenz. **Real Men Don't Eat Quiche.** New York: Pocket Books, 1992.

Fogle, Bruce. **ASPCA Complete Dog Care Manual.** New York: DK Publishing, 1993.

Hall, Lynn, and Antonio Castro. **Barry: The Bravest Saint Bernard.** New York: Random House, 1992.

Juniper, Dean Francis. **Man Against Mortality.** New York: Scribner, 1973.

Kay, William J., and Elizabeth Randolph. **The Complete Book of Dog Health.** Washington, D.C.: Howells House, 1990.

Landesman, Bill, and Kathleen Berman. **How to Care for Your Older Dog.** New York: F. Fell Publishers, 1978.

McGill, Michael. **The 40- to 60-Year-Old Male: A Guide for Men—and the Women in Their Lives—to See Them Through the Crises of the Male Middle Years.** New York: Simon & Schuster, 1980.

Mead, Shepherd. **Free the Male Man!** New York: Simon & Schuster, 1972.

Mellen, Joan. **Big Bad Wolves: Masculinity in the American Film.** New York: Pantheon, 1977.

Neville, Peter. **Do Dogs Need Shrinks?** Secaucus, N.J.: Citadel Press, 1992.

Patent, Dorothy Hinshaw. **Dogs: The Wolf Within (Understanding Animals).** Minneapolis: Carolrhoda Books, 1993.

Pesman, C. **How a Man Ages.** New York: Ballantine, 1984.

Ross, Geoffrey Aquilana. **How to Survive the Male Menopause.** London: Elm Tree Books, 1985.

Shoenberg, F. **Middle Age Rage—And Other Male Indignities.** New York: Simon & Schuster, 1987.

Sheehy, Gail. **Understanding Men's Passages: Discovering the New Map of Men's Lives.** New York: Random House, 1998.

Siegal, Mordecai, and Matthew Margolis. **When Good Dogs Do Bad Things.** Boston: Little, Brown, 1993.

White, Nancy. **Why Do Dogs Do That?** New York: Demco Media, 1995.

Wilkes, Paul. **Fitzgo: The Wild Dog of Central Park.** New York: Lippincott, 1973.

Woodhouse, Barbara. **No Bad Dogs: The Woodhouse Way.** New York: Summit Books, 1984.

Zilbergeld, Bernie. **The New Male Sexuality.** New York: Bantam, 1993.

{ARTICLES}

Galloway, J. **"New Tricks for Old Dogs."** *Runner's World* (June 1996): 40 (2).

Higham, T. **"Dances with Hounds"** *Sports Afield* (October 1992): 100 (2).

Liebman-Smith, J. **"Male Menopause: Fact or Fiction?"** *American Druggist* (April 1992): 18 (4).

Martin, R. **"In Praise of Old Dogs."** *Journal of Systems Management* (December 1994): 35 (2).

McFadden, C. **"Is There Really a Male Menopause?"** *New Choices for Retirement Living* (July 1994): 44 (5).

Morin, R. **"The Bald Truth."** *Washington Post* (17 November 1996): C5.

Perry, P. **"Teaching Dogs New Tricks."** *Saturday Evening Post* (November 1995): 44 (2).

Rader, E. **"Hello, Spare Tire!"** *Weight Watchers Magazine* (August 1988): 64 (2).

Rodman, S. **"Real Men Eat Tofu."** *Weight Watchers Magazine* (October 1989): 74 (2).

Rosenblatt, R. **"A Dog's Last Legs."** *Life* (March 1990): 19 (1).

Rundle, R. **"Hope for the Hairless."** *Wall Street Journal* (30 June 1995): B8.

Schwader, R. **"What Do Men Want? A Reading List for the Male Identity Crisis"** *New York Times Book Review* (9 January 1994): 3.

Sheehy, G. **"The Unspeakable Passage: Is There a Male Menopause?"** *Vanity Fair* (April 1993): 154 (13).

OTHER BOOKS OF INTEREST
FOR MEN AND THEIR DOGS

277 Secrets Your Dog Wants You to Know by Paulette Cooper

This revised edition reflects the latest in doggie knowledge and answers such timeless questions as, Should you vacuum your dog? and What can dogs hear, smell, and see—and should they watch TV? 208 pages.

Manhood: An Action Plan for Changing Men's Lives by Steve Biddulph

This insightful book tackles the six key areas of every man's life: resolving your relationship with your father, understanding love and sexuality, meeting your partner on equal terms, engaging actively with your children, finding meaning in your work, and freeing your wild spirit. 272 pages.

Rollo Bones, Canine Hypnotist by Marshall M. Moyer

Rollo is a soulful yellow dog who can hypnotize people with his big sad eyes. But when worldwide success threatens to turn what was once fun into drudgery, Rollo takes a stand. This wonderful children's book speaks to people of all ages who wish for a more peaceful life. 32 pages.

Fishing Dogs by Raymond Coppinger

This sly appraisal of the quirks of dog lovers, fishermen, and everyone in between introduces such heretofore unknown, but clearly essential, beasts as the Flounderhounder, the Stringer Spaniel, and many more. 128 pages.

Menopaws: The Silent Meow by Martha Sacks

The sister book to *Male Menopaws*, this full-color volume of gentle humor provides inspiration and playful coping strategies for the millions of women who are a bit apprehensive about the change of life. 64 pages.

Available from your local bookstore, or order direct from the publisher.
Call or write for our catalogs of over 900 books, posters, and tapes.

Ten Speed Press • Celestial Arts • Tricycle Press
Box 7123, Berkeley, California 94707
Order phone (800) 841-2665 • Fax (510) 559-1629 • order@tenspeed.com • www.tenspeedpress.com